The only thing harder than parenting a teen in this digital age is *being* a teen in this digital age. This calendar of creative and crucial tips for teens will help both parents and teenagers navigate our modern world with confidence.

One unanticipated consequence of personal technology devices is the crippling effect they can have on teen's ability to relate to others and be present in the world around them. With eyes down or headphones in much of the time, our teens miss important life lessons that would otherwise be picked up through daily interactions.

If that's not enough, our teens today are expected to figure out the dos and don'ts of an online presence and virtual connections without much guidance. There's a lot that needs to be taught deliberately to give them the best chance for success.

The good news? Teaching teens these tips can be simple and connective. Choose one tip per week to talk about and work on. Display the tip in your home or classroom, take a photo and text it to your kids, or if they prefer to learn on their own, let them read the calendar like a book. Each tip comes with helpful examples to illustrate each important point and ideas to get a discussion started.

Have younger kids at home? Great! Talking about these modern etiquette tips can be helpful and fun for the whole family. No one is too old or too young for self-reflection and improvement, and working together always beats a parent lecture (I promise, just ask your teen!).

If you are having trouble getting buy-in, just keep sharing and teaching. They might not act like they are listening, but they are learning more than they are willing to admit, and most really do want to create a life they are proud of — just maybe not while you are watching!

I can't wait to hear how these tips transform your home and prepare your kids and teens for a successful life in this modern world.

Love,
Brooke Romney

INTRODUCE YOURSELF

There are few things harder than being new or in a place where you don't know anyone. The ability to introduce yourself to strangers with confidence is something that will affect your life in a positive way for years to come. Remember, most people feel like outsiders, so anytime you can be the person who brings people together, you are a gift.

INTRODUCE YOURSELF.

IF YOU FIND YOURSELF
WITH PEOPLE YOU DON'T KNOW,
INTRODUCE YOURSELF.
YES, IT FEELS AWKWARD AT FIRST,
BUT IT GETS EASIER WITH PRACTICE.
IF YOU'RE NOT SURE WHERE TO START,
TRY, "I DON'T THINK I HAVE MET YOU YET.
I'M JANE. WHAT'S YOUR NAME?"
THIS IS A LIFE SKILL YOU WILL USE FOREVER.

PITCH IN

This tip is important in your own home and in the homes of others. If you are eating with another family, you can ask to set the table or cut a vegetable. Always clear your dishes and load them in the dishwasher. If you are at a group or school activity, don't leave before chairs and tables are put away. Don't be the one sitting while other people are working.

PITCH IN.

If food is being prepared
or an area is being cleaned,
ask what you can do to help.
Even better, just pitch in and fill a need.

A few minutes of help go a long way.

FIND NEW FRIENDS

Stop trying to fit in with people who don't appreciate you.

There are so many people who would love to have your personality, talent, and light in their life. Finding new friends is not easy, but the effort is worth it. You will have to put yourself out there and plan, invite, and probably be disappointed.

Look for those who might be a little lonely, new, or on the outside. These friends might be different from you or not have as much social clout but none of that matters if they are good people who enjoy and include you.

FIND NEW
FRIENDS.

IF YOUR FRIENDS ARE OFTEN EXCLUDING YOU OR MAKING YOU FEEL BAD, THEY ARE THE WRONG FRIENDS.

IF THIS HAPPENS CONSISTENTLY, START LOOKING FOR NEW FRIENDS. THIS IS NOT EASY. AT FIRST YOU MIGHT FEEL ALONE, BUT THERE ARE PEOPLE OUT THERE WHO WILL LIKE YOU FOR YOU. THESE NEW FRIENDS MIGHT NOT BE AS "COOL" OR YOUR FIRST CHOICE, BUT THAT'S OKAY. SPEND TIME WITH THOSE WHO TREAT YOU WELL AND WANT YOU AROUND.

BE THE FRIEND YOU WANT TO HAVE.

BE A GOOD PASSENGER

Being a teenager means you are going to need lots of rides.
You want to show gratitude to those who are willing to go
out of their way to get you where you need to be.
It's easy to use your cell phone as a way to escape from an
uncomfortable interaction, but it's not polite or gracious.
Make it a point to be a pleasant and grateful passenger.

BE A GOOD

PASSENGER.

WHEN SOMEONE GIVES YOU A RIDE, ACKNOWLEDGE THEM.

They are doing you a favor so say "hello"
and engage in a short conversation.
Be kind to everyone in the car.
Don't whisper or jump straight to your phone.
Always say "thank you" when you leave.

KEEP YOUR PHONE SILENT

Sometimes it's hard to resist the urge to do what is easiest for us, but no one wants to hear what you are watching, listening to, or talking about in a public place. If you don't have your headphones, watch without sound or wait until later. And yes, you might need to share this reminder with the adults in your life too!

KEEP YOUR PHONE SILENT.

IF YOU ARE IN A PUBLIC PLACE, YOUR PHONE SHOULD BE ON SILENT.

Use headphones; watch with subtitles; find a private spot; wait until later. Same rule goes for FaceTime, music, YouTube, memes, games, Netflix, Hulu and anything else that creates sound.

IN PUBLIC? SOUND OFF.

USE RESTAURANT MANNERS

These simple tips will help you be confident and comfortable when you go out to eat. You don't want to be the only person at the table who needs to ask your mom how you like your steak. Being kind and treating those serving you with respect is a sign of good character.

USE RESTAURANT MANNERS.

GREET YOUR SERVER WITH EYE CONTACT AND A SMILE.
SAY YOUR ORDER CLEARLY.
IF MENU ITEMS ARE UNFAMILIAR,
POLITELY ASK QUESTIONS TO CLARIFY.
ORDER PROMPTLY OR ASK FOR EXTRA TIME,
BUT DON'T LEAVE THE SERVER STANDING THERE WAITING.

KNOW IN ADVANCE HOW YOU LIKE YOUR MEAT AND EGGS COOKED.
WHEN YOUR FOOD IS SERVED, OR YOUR WATER IS REFILLED, SAY "THANK YOU."
DON'T BE SO LOUD OR DISRUPTIVE THAT YOU RUIN ANOTHER DINER'S EXPERIENCE.
PUT YOUR PHONES AWAY. TIDY UP THE TABLE AT THE END OF YOUR MEAL.
DON'T FORGET TO LEAVE A TIP.

TREAT YOUR FRIENDS' YOUNGER SIBLINGS WITH KINDNESS

When you are in someone else's home, you are a guest.

You should always be kind to all members of the family if you want to be welcomed back. Nothing is more endearing to parents than a teen treating younger siblings (even annoying ones) with kindness. Remember to keep language (swearing/slang), subject matter (mature/scary), shows, and music appropriate when they are around. If you think what you are doing, saying, listening to, or watching walks the line, wait until the littles are gone.

TREAT YOUR FRIENDS' YOUNGER SIBLINGS WITH KINDNESS.

INCLUDE THEM WHEN POSSIBLE AND ALWAYS BE AWARE OF AGE-APPROPRIATE LANGUAGE AND BEHAVIOR WHEN THEY ARE NEAR.

DON'T SHARE HURTFUL THINGS

You may think you are being the "good guy" by letting someone know they are being talked about, but you are usually just causing unnecessary drama. Everyone is human and people get bugged with each other and sometimes say things they shouldn't. It only blows up when that information is shared or spread, so don't be a part of it. Never bait others to get them to say or type something mean. The best thing you can do is be supportive and kind in words and texts and encourage others to do the same. If there is something significant being talked about that worries you, share it with a trusted adult to get help and perspective.

DON'T SHARE HURTFUL THINGS.

SHARING A SCREENSHOT OF AN UNKIND TEXT OR RETELLING SOMETHING RUDE YOU "HEARD" ABOUT A PERSON IS NOT BEING A GOOD FRIEND. EVEN IF YOUR INTENTIONS ARE GOOD, SHARING HURTFUL THINGS CAUSES PAIN TO EVERYONE INVOLVED AND PUTS YOU IN THE MIDDLE OF DRAMA.

IF IT IS HURTFUL, DON'T SHARE OR REPEAT IT.

THE WAY YOU SMELL MATTERS

Your hygiene is your responsibility. Being willing and able to take good care of your own body shows a lot of maturity. Being clean allows you to show up in the world confidently and allows others to be close to you without being offended or turned off. Simple habits, started early, are extremely valuable.

If you have questions or need supplies, feel free to ask!

THE WAY YOU SMELL
MATTERS.

BRUSH YOUR TEETH EVERY MORNING AND NIGHT.
FLOSS AND USE MOUTHWASH.
HAVE GUM OR MINTS ON HAND.
DEODORANT IS A MUST, EVERYDAY.
DAILY SHOWERS AND WASHING WITH SOAP ARE NON-NEGOTIABLE.
YOU MIGHT EVEN NEED TO SHOWER MORE THAN ONCE.
WASH YOUR HAIR REGULARLY. HAIR AND SCALPS HAVE ODOR TOO.
PERFUME, COLOGNE, AND BODY SPRAY ARE OKAY
(IN SMALL AMOUNTS), BUT THEY DON'T MASK STINK.

DON'T LEAVE JUST ONE PERSON OUT

You can't always invite everyone to everything, but there is almost always room for one more. If you have a group of ten friends, having five over is fine, but never invite nine and leave out one person. Don't create new group messages that exclude one friend or plan something and tell only one person they aren't invited. Don't use your power to make others miserable. Surely you don't want to be remembered as the person who made people feel small, unwanted, or hopeless. Think outside yourself and beyond the moment.

DON'T LEAVE JUST ONE PERSON OUT.

INVITING ALL EXCEPT ONE
IS CRUEL. BE SOMEONE WHO
INCLUDES AND MAKES ROOM.
IF YOU HAVE A PROBLEM
WITH SOMEONE, TALK TO THEM;
DON'T JUST GHOST THEM.
PUT YOURSELF IN THAT PERSON'S
SHOES BECAUSE CHANCES ARE,
YOU WILL BE LEFT OUT SOMEDAY.

REMEMBER:
THERE IS ALWAYS ROOM FOR ONE MORE.

MAKE AND MANAGE
YOUR OWN APPOINTMENTS

Be comfortable voicing what you would like when it comes to your hair. Bring a photo, communicate clearly, and engage in polite conversation. When it comes to dentists and doctors, advocate for yourself. Share your concerns honestly and clearly. Get a second opinion if you aren't satisfied or don't feel taken seriously. Prepare questions or take notes if necessary. If you like the person who helped you, write their name down so you can request them in the future.

MAKE AND MANAGE —— YOUR OWN APPOINTMENTS. ——

HAVE YOUR CALENDAR READY WHEN YOU CALL.
ARRIVE A FEW MINUTES EARLY.
IF YOU CAN'T MAKE IT,
CANCEL 24 HOURS IN ADVANCE.
WHEN YOU GET TO THE APPOINTMENT,
KNOW WHAT HAIRCUT TO REQUEST
OR HOW TO TALK TO A PHYSICIAN
ABOUT YOUR CONCERNS.

GIVE THEM YOUR FULL ATTENTION.
PUT YOUR PHONE AWAY UNLESS YOU ARE USING IT TO TAKE NOTES.
SAY THANK YOU AS YOU LEAVE.

DECLINE KINDLY

Saying "no" to an invitation is often uncomfortable, even for adults, but being upfront and honest is so much kinder than just ignoring or avoiding someone.

Having a few "go to" phrases can be really helpful.

When you are on the other end of this and doing the inviting, isn't it better to just know that someone can't come?

DECLINE KINDLY.

DON'T IGNORE PEOPLE.
IF YOU CAN'T MAKE IT, JUST LET THEM KNOW.

TRY USING ONE OF THE FOLLOWING OPTIONS
OR COME UP WITH YOUR OWN:

"Thanks so much for the invite.
I am sad I can't make it."

"Sounds like so much fun.
I wish I didn't already have plans."

"Darn! That night doesn't work for me.
Can we get together next weekend?"

BE ON TIME

Planning your life so you can be punctual is a critical skill. It shows good time management, responsibility, and consideration for others. Being late happens on occasion and everyone understands, but give people a heads up when you can and thank them for their patience. If being late is habitual, see if there is something you need to change (wake up time, realistic drive time, etc.) that can help you be more on time. Remember that EVERYONE'S time is valuable, not just yours.

BE ON TIME.

PLAN YOUR LIFE SO YOU CAN BE PUNCTUAL.

Set reminders or alarms.
Keep a schedule.
If you are going to be late,
let those waiting know as soon as possible.
Thank others for waiting for you when you arrive.

NOTHING ONLINE IS PRIVATE

Writing from behind a screen gives you a false sense of security, but it shouldn't! In fact, there is good reason to be even MORE careful online. With the ability to screenshot anything, even things you thought would disappear never really do and proof of it can stick around forever. So, before you post it, text it, or send it, be sure that if the entire world saw it or if it got brought up by a future employer, you would be okay to own that picture or those words.

NOTHING ONLINE IS PRIVATE.

IF YOU WOULD NOT BE OKAY WITH YOUR PARENTS, THEIR PARENTS, THE ENTIRE SCHOOL, OR A FUTURE EMPLOYER SEEING OR READING IT, KEEP IT TO YOURSELF. NOTHING ONLINE EVER REALLY GOES AWAY, AND IN OUR DIGITAL WORLD, NOTHING IS PRIVATE.

BE AWARE

Mental health is serious and it is important to check in on your friends. Notice when someone suddenly disappears, harms themselves, or talks about suicide.

There is a fine line between tattling and looking out for someone, but it is an important one. If something concerning is going on, it is usually too big for teens to handle on their own and a trusted adult needs to be involved so the right help can be provided.

BE AWARE.

IF YOU ARE CONCERNED, SPEAK UP!
IF A FRIEND IS ACTING STRANGE,
SENDS A TROUBLING TEXT,
IS HURTING THEMSELVES OR OTHERS,
OR WITHDRAWS FROM NORMAL
ACTIVITY, TELL A TRUSTED
ADULT. THERE ARE EVEN WAYS
TO DO THIS ANONYMOUSLY.

THESE ACTIONS CAN CHANGE A PAINFUL PATH OR EVEN SAVE A LIFE.

ACKNOWLEDGE ADULTS

Cell phones have made it really easy to never have to interact with the parents in a home, but just because it is easier doesn't mean that it is right. Always acknowledge the adults in the home. Something simple like, "Hi, Mrs. Smith. Thanks for letting me come over!" is great. If someone has allowed you to spend all evening at their house, make sure you say "thank you" and "goodbye" before you leave.

ACKNOWLEDGE ADULTS.

WHEN YOU WALK
INTO A HOME OR
LEAVE A HOME,
ACKNOWLEDGE THE ADULTS
WHO ARE THERE.
DON'T JUST
SNEAK IN AND OUT.
SAY "HELLO," "GOODBYE," AND
"THANK YOU."
BONUS POINTS FOR
HAVING A
CONVERSATION.

TAKE OWNERSHIP OF YOUR MISTAKES

Shifting blame to others is natural, but it's not a very productive way to live. Instead of blaming a coach for your lack of playing time, figure out what you can improve to get the results you want. Instead of blaming a loss on a referee, look at what you could have done in the game to change the outcome. Instead of blaming a teacher for a poor grade, notice where you have fallen short. Realize that you have the power to make better choices and get better outcomes. Every now and then, something truly is unfair, which is also part of life. If you see a real gap or problem, work for solutions instead of just complaining.

TAKE OWNERSHIP OF YOUR
MISTAKES.

IN A SITUATION THAT HASN'T GONE WELL, TAKE RESPONSIBILITY
FOR YOUR PART. DON'T GIVE EXCUSES. DON'T BLAME THE REFEREE
OR THE COACH. DON'T PLACE THE BURDEN ON A FRIEND.
DON'T DECIDE IT WAS THE TEACHER'S FAULT.
ACKNOWLEDGE HOW YOU CONTRIBUTED TO THE PROBLEM
AND HOW YOU CAN DO BETTER IN THE FUTURE.

APOLOGIZE RIGHT

When you are in the wrong, it is much more comfortable to justify what happened by making excuses or shifting the blame, but that is not an apology. When you apologize be sincere, take ownership, and figure out how to make amends. This can save relationships when done correctly.

APOLOGIZE RIGHT.

IF YOU HAVE DONE SOMETHING WRONG OR HURTFUL, LEARN TO APOLOGIZE SINCERELY WITHOUT BLAMING THE OTHER PERSON OR GIVING EXCUSES.

"I am really sorry I did _____ . I feel really bad about it. I hope you can forgive me but I understand it might take some time. What can I do to make it up to you?"

RESPECT PEOPLE'S HOMES

It is easy to feel comfortable in other's homes or to assume that every home has the same rules as your own, but every family is different. It's better to err on the side of caution until you really get to know someone. Asking simple questions about house rules can make a big difference and guarantee that you are welcome any time.

RESPECT PEOPLE'S HOMES.

ASK ABOUT THEIR SHOE POLICY.
NEVER PUT YOUR FEET ON FURNITURE.
DON'T LIE ON DECORATIVE PILLOWS.
ASK PERMISSION BEFORE EATING.
KEEP YOUR FOOD AND DRINKS IN THE KITCHEN.
STAY IN COMMON AREAS AND OUT OF BEDROOMS.
IF YOU MESS IT UP, CLEAN IT UP.
KEEP YOUR VOLUME AT AN APPROPRIATE LEVEL.
IF YOU BREAK SOMETHING, TAKE RESPONSIBILITY
AND REPLACE IT.

KNOW YOURSELF

This is a question you will be asked the rest of your life, so having an answer is a useful plan. At certain times of life the answer will be quick and easy, and at other times it might take more thought. Just remember: you don't have to be great at something to love it or love something to be interested in it. You don't need to have others' approval for what you find motivating or exciting and you can change what you love as many times as you want!

KNOW YOURSELF.

When someone asks you what you like to do or what you are into, have an answer ready. There is no "right answer" to this question, but "I don't know" or "nothing" is the wrong answer. You don't have to be awesome at something to be interested in it. You don't have to be on a team or in a club to have a hobby. What you love doesn't have to be loved by everyone else. If you don't know what to say, take some time to think about it. If no answer comes, try more things.

BE INCLUSIVE

You want to make others feel welcome — only focusing on one or two people in a group does the opposite of that. Remember, what is most comfortable for you can sometimes make others feel excluded. Only focusing on one or two people you know or like can alienate the rest of the group or interrupt a conversation. You can still create space for yourself by introducing yourself to the whole group. If you really only know or want to talk with one person, say hi quickly and ask them to come find you when they are finished with their current conversation.

BE INCLUSIVE.

WHEN WALKING UP TO A GROUP
OF PEOPLE, ACKNOWLEDGE
EVERYONE THERE — NOT JUST
ONE PERSON. DON'T JUST INSERT
YOURSELF AND BLOCK OTHERS
OR PULL ONE OR TWO PEOPLE
AWAY FROM THE GROUP.
IF YOU DON'T KNOW EVERYONE,
INTRODUCE YOURSELF.

FRIENDSHIP TAKES TIME AND WORK

We live in a world of instant gratification where we can have almost anything we want instantaneously, but this study from the University of Kansas proves that friendship isn't like that. If you want to build strong bonds, you have to put in the time. Be patient as you grow relationships.

https://news.ku.edu/2018/03/06/study-reveals-number-hours-it-takes-make-friend

FRIENDSHIP
TAKES TIME AND WORK.

IT TAKES 40-60 HOURS TO FORM A CASUAL FRIENDSHIP;
80-100 HOURS TO TRANSITION TO A FRIEND; AND MORE
THAN 200 HOURS TO BECOME GOOD FRIENDS.

DON'T BE IMPATIENT WHEN IT COMES TO
QUALITY CONNECTION.

LEARN PHONE MANNERS

While actual phone conversations are more rare than they used to be, it is still important to have good manners. Always speak clearly so the person on the other line can understand you and remember to end the conversation — don't just hang up on someone.

LEARN—
PHONE MANNERS.

SAY
"HELLO"
WHEN YOU
ANSWER THE
PHONE AND
"GOODBYE"
WHEN A
CONVERSATION
IS OVER.

LAND A JOB

Getting hired for a job is an important part of growing up. Doing each step for yourself will give you self confidence and independence. Use your contacts and connections when job hunting. You have the best chance of getting hired if you make the right impression every step of the way. Make sure your email address and voicemail message are adult appropriate. If you are hired, be a hard worker and reliable employee.

LAND A JOB.

When applying for a job, do it right. Double check
your application to make sure your email address and
phone number are correct. Check your voicemail regularly
(and be sure it isn't full!) so you can get back to the
manager in a timely manner. At every stage of the process,
dress appropriately and be polite and friendly.
Practice your interviewing skills,
make eye contact, and speak clearly. Keep your phone
put away. If you accept a job, make sure you are available
to fulfill your duties.

YOU ATTRACT WHAT YOU PUT INTO THE WORLD

You often get what you give, so if you don't like what is coming into your life, change what you're putting out there.

As you make small improvements, notice the difference in yourself and those around you.

Remember that the only person you can change is you.

YOU ATTRACT WHAT YOU PUT INTO THE WORLD.

IF YOU WANT MORE POSITIVITY,
BE MORE POSITIVE.

IF YOU WANT FRIENDS WHO LIFT YOU,
START LIFTING OTHERS.

IF YOU WISH THE WORLD WAS KINDER,
START WITH YOURSELF.

IF YOU CAN'T STAND DRAMA,
STOP FEEDING INTO IT.

IF YOU WANT MORE GOODNESS,
BE THE GOOD.

ANSWER THE DOOR POLITELY

Welcoming guests to your home in a polite and kind manner is an important way to show you care. Even if the guest is a friend of a sibling or someone you know well, practice good manners and common courtesy.

ANSWER THE DOOR POLITELY.

GREET THE PERSON STANDING THERE. IF THEY ARE SOMEONE YOU KNOW WELL, INVITE THEM IN. QUICKLY FIND THE PERSON THEY ARE ASKING TO SEE. MAKE POLITE CONVERSATION UNTIL THE PERSON THEY NEED ARRIVES.

BE A GREAT HOUSEGUEST

Being able to stay in someone's home for an extended period of time is such a wonderful service! It saves so much money, hassle, and time on your part. It also creates a lot of extra work and stress for the host, so be sure to acknowledge that kindness and effort. Always respect the space and home rules of the place you are staying. If you don't know what they are, just ask! Be gracious and appreciative by looking for ways to help out when you can ... meal prep, dishes, asking if anything is needed when you are out. Keep your areas clean and organized and leave your space as put together as possible, even deep clean as much as you can before you go.

Always send a thank you note or a small gift to show your appreciation!

BE A GREAT
HOUSEGUEST.

IF YOU ARE STAYING IN SOMEONE'S HOME, ARRIVE WITH A SMALL
HOSTESS GIFT. MAKE YOUR BED AND KEEP YOUR ROOM TIDY, EVEN
IF YOU AREN'T USUALLY THAT WAY AT HOME. KEEP THE BATHROOM
CLEAN SO OTHERS CAN ALSO USE IT. SPEND SOME TIME WITH
YOUR HOST. ASK ABOUT KITCHEN RULES AND NEEDS.
HELP WITH MEAL PREP. BEFORE YOU LEAVE, ASK WHAT YOU CAN DO
WITH YOUR SHEETS AND TOWELS, TAKE YOUR GARBAGE OUT, AND
WIPE EVERYTHING DOWN. SEND A SINCERE THANK YOU NOTE
AND MAYBE A GIFT YOU CAN AFFORD AFTER YOUR STAY.

SPEAK WITH CONFIDENCE

To communicate effectively, it is important that the other person understands what you are saying. You can do your part by speaking clearly and confidently. This might take some practice, but the end result is worth it.

SPEAK WITH CONFIDENCE.

IF YOU HAVE SOMETHING TO SAY, SAY IT WITH CONFIDENCE.

Look people in the eye.

Don't mumble.

Enunciate your words.

Speak loudly and clearly enough
for people to hear and understand.

BE PRESENT

With near-constant distractions on our phone, it can be difficult to be present, but it is a healthy habit to practice. Being present will allow you to more fully enjoy the life you are living and value the people around you. Put your phone on silent or turn off notifications when you are with people. Plan to check your phone at set times instead of being on it constantly. If you are waiting for an important text, let people know.

BE
PRESENT.

IF YOU ARE IN A ROOM
WITH PEOPLE, THEY TAKE
PRIORITY OVER WHATEVER IS
HAPPENING ON YOUR PHONE.
DON'T SCROLL WHILE WATCHING
A MOVIE OR SNAP OTHER
GROUPS WHILE HANGING
OUT WITH YOUR OWN.
CHOOSE TO BE ENGAGED
AND ENJOY WHAT/WHO IS IN
FRONT OF YOU INSTEAD
OF WONDERING WHAT ELSE
IS GOING ON. THIS WILL HELP
YOU CONNECT AND BUILD
STRONGER RELATIONSHIPS.

MAKE A GREAT FIRST IMPRESSION

Nothing is quite as important as a first impression,

so they are to be taken seriously.

Make the best one possible by knowing how to confidently

introduce yourself. This might feel awkward or take a little

practice, but it's a simple skill to learn.

MAKE A GREAT FIRST

IMPRESSION.

When you meet someone,
shake their hand firmly,
smile, look them in the eye,
and say, "Hi. My name is Jane.
Nice to meet you."
Practice with family members
so when the time comes,
you are ready.

SAY THANK YOU

There are a lot of people in this world who go out of their way to help you.
Expressing gratitude to them on a regular basis makes them feel appreciated
and more willing to help you in the future. A grateful life is a much happier
life, so notice the small things people do for you and say thanks!

SAY THANK YOU.

Vocalize your appreciation frequently,
especially to teachers, coaches, tutors,
servers, or others who help you.
Do it often enough that it becomes a habit.

HOLD DOORS OPEN

Walking through life with your eyes up will allow you to see needs.

If you get to a door first, hold it open for the people coming in

behind you. If you see someone pushing a stroller or wheelchair,

go out of your way to get the door for them.

Small acts of service like this can make the world a better, kinder place.

HOLD DOORS OPEN.

If there is someone entering behind you, kindly hold the door open, especially if they have their hands full.

DON'T WHISPER

When two people start to whisper in a group setting, it changes the dynamic and dulls the fun. Immediately others begin to feel self-conscious, left out, and feelings get hurt. Think of how you feel when those around you begin to whisper.

It's uncomfortable, right?

You don't want others to feel that way.

Not every conversation is meant for a group, but if you can't say it in front of everyone, wait for a better time.

DON'T WHISPER.

WHISPERING IN FRONT OF OTHERS IS NOT OKAY.
FIND A MORE APPROPRIATE PLACE AND TIME
TO HAVE PRIVATE CONVERSATIONS.

FIND A CODE WORD

Sometimes teenagers are put in situations that don't feel right. The adults who care about you want to do whatever they can to keep you as safe as possible. Come up with a word or phrase that you use in a text or phone call that can signal you are unsafe or worried about what might happen next. You can always use adults as an excuse to get out of a tricky situation.

FIND A
CODE WORD.

DECIDE ON A CODE WORD WITH YOUR PARENTS THAT YOU CAN TEXT OR USE IN A PHONE CALL IF YOU ARE EVER IN A SITUATION THAT DOESN'T FEEL RIGHT OR SAFE. MAKE A PLAN FOR WHEN THAT WORD IS COMMUNICATED.

SAY NO TO RATING GAMES

Rating games can seem silly and harmless, but they aren't. They have been the cause of a lot of dark thoughts, damaged feelings, plummeting self-esteem, and even school suspensions. Let's work on seeing people for who they really are, not just what they look like.

Refusing to play these games is a good first step.

If you feel strong enough to stop them, that is even better.

SAY NO TO
RATINGS.

RATING PEOPLE'S LOOKS OR BODIES IS NEVER APPROPRIATE AND ALWAYS ENDS UP BEING HURTFUL. NEVER ASK SOMEONE TO RATE YOU. BELIEVE YOU ARE MUCH MORE THAN AN ARBITRARY NUMBER. IF YOU SEE THIS HAPPENING ON AN APP OR IN PERSON, DON'T PARTICIPATE.

BE TRUSTWORTHY

Friendship is built on trust and if you are constantly breaking that trust,

it will be hard to keep a friend.

There are times when a secret needs to be shared to keep people safe,

but that's rare. Be the kind of trustworthy and loyal person you would like

to have in your corner.

BE TRUSTWORTHY.

IF A FRIEND TELLS YOU
SOMETHING IN CONFIDENCE,
KEEP THEIR SECRET
UNLESS YOU ARE
WORRIED ABOUT THEIR
SAFETY OR THE
SAFETY OF SOMEONE ELSE.
BEING TRUSTWORTHY
IS CRUCIAL TO FRIENDSHIP.

BE A GOOD LISTENER

There are few good listeners in our world today, so having this skill can really set you apart. Good listeners are better learners, better friends, and better employees. They allow others to feel valued and can facilitate understanding. Really listening isn't always easy or natural, but it is worth practicing.

BE A GOOD
LISTENER.

Active listening is more than just opening your ears.
Face the speaker. Put your phone down.
Make eye contact. Nod. Don't interrupt.
Don't judge or jump to conclusions.
Don't start planning what to say next.
Stay focused. Ask questions.
Paraphrase or summarize what someone has said
so you are sure you understand.

KEEP PRIVATE INFORMATION PRIVATE

It is really easy to pretend to be someone you are not online.

Just because someone claims to be a 14-year-old girl doesn't mean they really

are. They could be hiding behind a fake picture and teenage slang, so learn to

be on the defensive and protect yourself. Don't accept messages or requests

from people you don't know and keep your accounts private. If there is

something online that makes you feel uncomfortable, tell a trusted adult.

Many online relationships that start off innocently end badly.

KEEP PRIVATE INFORMATION

PRIVATE.

DO NOT TALK TO OR COMMUNICATE WITH PEOPLE ONLINE
YOU DO NOT KNOW. DO NOT GIVE OUT YOUR ADDRESS,
AGE, SCHOOL NAME, PHONE NUMBER, ETC.
PEOPLE ARE NOT ALWAYS WHO THEY SEEM TO BE.

DO YOUR PART

When everyone contributes, the load is much lighter all around.

When it comes to work ethic, you can get a reputation quickly—

a good one can lead you to endless opportunities.

At a bare minimum, do your part and when you can, do more.

You will reap rewards from being a person others can count on.

DO YOUR PART.

If you are participating in a group project,
pull your weight.
If you are assigned a job at home or work,
do it well.
Don't shirk responsibilities or wait for
someone else to pick up your slack.

TALK ABOUT MONEY
IN APPROPRIATE WAYS

Talking about money isn't always bad, but being intrusive or braggy about it isn't okay. If you have a serious question about money, ask your parents or a teacher. If you want to share a good deal with a friend, do it! If you are looking for a job and are curious about the starting salaries, ask people privately if they are comfortable sharing. Make sure those in your life know that their value has nothing to do with what is in their wallet.

TALK ABOUT ———— MONEY IN APPROPRIATE WAYS. ————

DON'T ASK SOMEONE HOW MUCH THEIR PARENTS MAKE OR HOW MUCH THEIR HOUSE/CAR COST. IT IS NOT POLITE TO ANNOUNCE HOW PRICEY YOUR SHOES ARE OR HOW MUCH YOU PAID FOR YOUR DRESS. NO ONE'S WORTH IS MEASURED BY HOW MUCH THEY HAVE IN THE BANK.

FOCUS ON THINGS THAT ARE MORE IMPORTANT.

LET GO OF CONTROL

So much of our frustration in life happens when others don't do or say or act the way you hoped they would. Life is infinitely happier when you stop trying to control people and focus your energy on creating the life you would like to have.

LET GO OF CONTROL.

The only person you can really control is yourself. Don't waste your time trying to control others or being frustrated when they don't do what you hoped they would. Focus on what you can control and let go of the rest.

WATCH YOUR BODY LANGUAGE

If people often get the wrong idea about who you are,

it may be because of your tone, expression, or body language.

Sometimes these things stand out more than words do.

Being open to feedback can help you make small adjustments

that improve your relationships, confidence, and allow you

to be more comfortable being yourself.

WATCH YOUR BODY
LANGUAGE.

VOICE TONE, FACIAL EXPRESSIONS, AND BODY LANGUAGE
ARE CRUCIAL TO HOW YOU ARE RECEIVED IN THIS WORLD.
MAKE SURE YOUR TONE ISN'T HARSH WHEN YOU SPEAK.
DON'T CONSTANTLY LOOK MAD WHEN YOU AREN'T OR
SEEM STUCK UP OR UNAPPROACHABLE WHEN YOU REALLY
ARE OPEN AND INCLUSIVE. ASK THOSE WHO LOVE YOU HOW
YOU COME ACROSS AND BE WILLING TO LISTEN AND IMPROVE.
THERE IS NOTHING WRONG WITH BEING YOU!
JUST MAKE SURE WHO YOU ARE ON THE OUTSIDE MATCHES
WHO YOU ARE ON THE INSIDE.

PRACTICE BOREDOM

Being bored is crucial for your brain: it sparks solutions, helps recharge your mental health, allows you to discover new hobbies, clarifies thoughts, and cultivates mindfulness. Adding a few minutes of boredom to your day adds all kinds of positive benefits.

PRACTICE BOREDOM.

Challenge yourself to have screen-free time daily without being antsy or agitated. Allow yourself time each week to think without any external input. Being comfortable in silence and without distractions is a skill that pays dividends when it comes to peace, self-reflection, and creativity.

OPEN YOUR EARS

This is a simple way to show the people you are with that you care

about them and value your time together.

Do your best to remember to take ear buds out in social settings.

OPEN YOUR EARS.

WHEN YOU'RE WITH OTHER PEOPLE, YOUR HEADPHONES OR AIRPODS SHOULD NOT BE IN YOUR EARS. IT DOESN'T MATTER IF THEY ARE ON, OFF, OR TURNED DOWN, THEY SHOULD BE PUT AWAY IN THE COMPANY OF OTHERS. SAVE THEM FOR A TIME WHEN YOU ARE ALONE.

ADVOCATE FOR YOURSELF AT SCHOOL

It's important that you learn to take control of your education.

You are smart and capable of having important conversations.

Parents only need to be involved if you have tried and are being

ignored or misunderstood.

ADVOCATE FOR YOURSELF AT SCHOOL.

IF YOU DON'T UNDERSTAND SOMETHING, ASK A QUESTION. IF YOU THINK AN ANSWER IS RIGHT THAT WAS MARKED WRONG, KINDLY APPROACH THE TEACHER TO ASK FOR CLARIFICATION. IF YOU NEED AN EXTENSION ON AN ASSIGNMENT OR ARE LOOKING FOR EXTRA CREDIT, PRACTICE HAVING THOSE CONVERSATIONS SO YOU COME ACROSS CLEAR AND APPRECIATIVE.

BE RELIABLE

It can be exceptionally difficult to keep your plans with someone when a better, more fun, or cooler offer comes up, but choose to be a good friend. You can ask your friend if they are open to a new plan and try to combine groups, but that won't always work. Ditching out for something better is selfish and hurtful. Remember to treat others as you would want to be treated.

BE
RELIABLE.

If you make plans with someone, keep them,
even if you get a better offer.

SHARE THE LAST ONE

There is a constant battle between selfishness and generosity inside our heads, but choosing to think of others is always a good thing. Often, no one will mind if you take the last of something, but it is always appropriate to be considerate and willing to share.

SHARE THE LAST ONE.

If there is only one of something left and you want it,
ask if anyone else would like it before you take it.
This goes for the last piece of pizza, the only
slice of cake, or the last roll in the restaurant basket.
This is important in both home and social settings.
Be aware of others and think outside of yourself.

WORDS MATTER

Just because we don't want someone to be offended by what we say doesn't mean they won't be. If you have to preface what you are saying with these phrases, it may not be something that needs to be shared. If it is important and needs to be said, make sure you are sharing it with love and in an appropriate setting.

WORDS
MATTER.

The words, "no offense" or "not to be rude" do not mean that what comes next will not be hurtful to the person you are saying it to. In fact, if you feel a need to say these phrases, think twice about saying anything at all.

EXPRESS GRATITUDE

When people go out of their way to spend money or time on you, be sure to let them know how grateful you are. This is best done by a handwritten thank you note, but if that isn't a possibility or something you will get around to, shoot off a sincere text right away to let them know you received and loved it.

EXPRESS GRATITUDE.

If you receive a gift, send a thank you note or,
at a minimum, a heartfelt text.

REPLY

It is so much easier (and more respectful) to reply right away than it is to wait for that reminder text. If you don't know the answer to something, just let them know you will get back to them. This wouldn't be a bad thing to adopt with your friends either.

No one likes to be ignored.

REPLY.

WHEN AN ADULT TEXTS YOU, YOU NEED TO REPLY.
RARELY DO ADULTS TEXT TEENS JUST TO CHITCHAT;
THEY ARE ALMOST ALWAYS PASSING ON INFORMATION.
EVEN A THUMBS UP TO LET THEM KNOW YOU GOT THE
MESSAGE WORKS. IF THEY ARE ASKING A QUESTION, NEED
A HEAD COUNT, OR A RESPONSE, MAKE SURE YOU GIVE IT
TO THEM, THEN THEY DON'T HAVE TO KEEP PESTERING YOU.

SHARE YOUR SEAT

If you are in a crowded area, on public transportation, or in a venue with limited seating, look around and see if there is someone who needs your seat more than you do and kindly offer it to them.

SHARE
YOUR SEAT.

IF SEATING IS SCARCE, OFFER UP YOUR SEAT TO THE ELDERLY OR THOSE WHO LOOK LIKE THEY NEED A PLACE TO REST MORE THAN YOU DO.

GET PERMISSION

Everyone has different levels of comfort when it comes to their online footprint. Before you post about someone, make sure they are okay with the words and the photo. Don't be the person that embarrasses others online or makes them feel uncomfortable because of what you post. And never be the person who posts or reposts inappropriate things.

GET PERMISSION.

BEFORE POSTING A PHOTO OR
EXPERIENCE ABOUT SOMEONE,
GET THEIR PERMISSION.
RESPECTING PRIVACY IS IMPORTANT.
NEVER POST ANYTHING
INAPPROPRIATE OF ANYONE, EVER.

www.BrookeRomney.com

Printed in China

First Edition

10 9 8

Library of Congress data has been applied for.

ISBN 978-1-7358544-3-4

About the Author

Brooke Romney is a writer, speaker, educator and connector. She has been published in *The Washington Post, The Deseret News,* and a host of other online publications where her pieces have been read millions of times. In October 2020, she published her first book, *I Like Me Anyway: Embracing Imperfection, Connection, and Christ,* which has changed the lives and perspective of thousands of women and men all over the world.

This book, *52 Modern Manners for Today's Teens,* was born from raising her own teens in a newly digital world and the questions and responses she received from many in her personal and online communities. She hopes this book allows both teens and parents a fresh perspective and doable strategies for living a more successful and connected life.

If this book has been helpful for you or your teen, please consider leaving a review on Amazon so it is more easily discovered by others. Reviews and genuine sharing in person or on social media are the most wonderful gifts you can give to a self-published author.

You can find more of Brooke's work on her website, BrookeRomney.com and her instagram @brookeromneywrites where she loves connecting and learning daily. She hopes to see you there!

HAS THIS BOOK SPARKED MORE MODERN MANNERS?
ADD YOUR EXTRA ONES BELOW!